GUILDFORD TO REDHILL

Vic Mitchell and Keith Smith

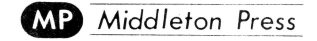

MP *Middleton Press*

Cover picture:
A Train of typical SECR stock waits at the gas-lit down platform of Betchworth station on 9th November 1935, while wagons stand in the siding to the nearby limeworks. The locomotive is ex-SECR 4-4-0 class F1 no. 1240. (H.C. Casserley)

134 3556

0906520630020 /

METROPOLITAN BOROUGH
OF WIRRAL
DEPT. OF LEISURE SERVICES
LIBRARIES AND ARTS DIVISION

SBN ACC.N. 0906520630	
LOC. COPY BI 02.	Y.P.
CLASS No. 385.09422I HIT.	

HT 712480

Design – Deborah Goodridge

First published March 1989

ISBN 0 906520 63 0

© *Middleton Press, 1988*

Typeset by CitySet - Bosham 573270

*Published by Middleton Press
     Easebourne Lane
     Midhurst, West Sussex
     GU29 9AZ
     ☎ (073 081) 3169*

*Printed & bound by Biddles Ltd,
     Guildford and Kings Lynn*

ACKNOWLEDGEMENTS

In addition to many of the photographers credited in the captions, we have received valuable assistance from R.M. Casserley, Prof. & Mrs. A. Crocker, G. Croughton, J.R.W. Kirkby, J.D. Knight, H.N. James, N. Langridge, J. Lunn, D. Pede, R. Randell, D.H. Smith, E. Staff and N. Stanyon. We are very grateful for this help and also for the support and meticulous work of our wives.

CONTENTS

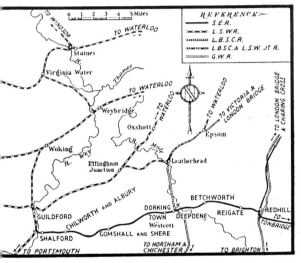

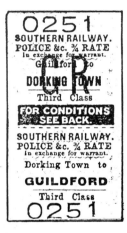

Map to show nineteenth century ownership of railways in the area. (Railway Magazine)

Gradient profile, showing mileage from Reading.

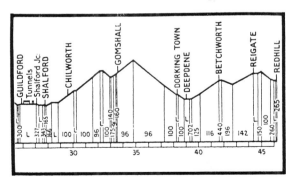

GEOGRAPHICAL SETTING

Guildford is strategically set in the Wey Gap in the North Downs and the entire route runs roughly parallel to these chalk hills. South of this market town, the line runs close to the River Wey and is carried in tunnels through the chalk and the parallel sandy ridge of the Folkestone Beds.

Turning east, the railway follows the valley of the River Tillingbourne, apart from one deviation south to cross the Hythe Beds of Albury Heath. After this the line descends into the valley again, near Gomshall. A further climb takes the route over the watershed to the catchment area of the River Mole, which is crossed east of Dorking. From the summit to Betchworth, the line was built on the narrow outcrop of Upper Greensand, which runs along the foot of the North Downs. In this area, the geology was of economic importance for many years, for the production of lime and hearthstone. The parallel outcrop of Gault Clay gave rise to rail traffic associated with brickmaking.

The remainder of the route is mainly over the sands of the Folkestone Beds and ends at 250 ft. above sea level, double the height at which it started at Guildford.

The maps in this album are to the scale of 25″ to 1 mile, unless otherwise stated.

HISTORICAL BACKGROUND

The first railway in the area was the London – Brighton line, which was opened between Croydon and Haywards Heath on 12th July 1841. This later became part of the London, Brighton & South Coast Railway, although used by Dover trains of the South Eastern Railway as far south as Redhill (then Reigate Junction).

In the west, the London & South Western Railway opened a branch to Guildford, from its London – Southampton main line, on 5th May 1845. The branch was extended to Godalming on 15th October 1849 and another was opened between Guildford and Farnham on 8th October 1849.

On 4th July 1849, the SER started to operate trains on the Reading, Guildford & Reigate Railway between Redhill and Dorking (now Dorking West). The service was extended west to Shalford on 20th August 1849 and to Guildford and Reading on 15th October of the same year. This necessitated using LSWR tracks between Shalford Junction and Ash Junction. In 1852, the SER purchased the RG&RR, which had received its Act of Parliament in 1846.

The LBSCR provided Dorking with a more direct service to London when its Horsham – Leatherhead route was opened in 1867. All the lines became part of the Southern Railway in 1923 and British Railways in 1948.

Electrification of the Redhill – Reigate section took place on 17th July 1932, being part of the Purley – Three Bridges section of the Brighton scheme. Guildford – Shalford Junction electrification took place on 4th July 1937, when the Portsmouth Direct line was energised for traffic. Hopes are high that the remainder of the route will be electrified to handle some of the Channel Tunnel traffic and that local services will benefit accordingly. Prior to WWI, the SECR proposed the use of electric locomotives but the N class was produced instead. Several more electrification schemes have been produced but a successful one is still awaited.

PASSENGER SERVICES

Departures from Redhill

	WEEKDAYS			SUNDAYS	
Guildford or beyond	Dorking Town only	Gomshall only	Guildford or beyond	Dorking Town only	Gomshall only
1849	5	1		3	1	
1869	5	8		2	2	
1890	11	4		3	1	
1906	13	4	2	4	3	1
1914	12	4	1	4	3	2
1917	9	2		4	1	
1921	15	3	2	4		1
1928	14	3	3	4		2
1934	18		4	10		1
1938	19		4	10		1
1944	15	1		9		
1948	15			8		
1954	16	1		10		
1958	15	1		10		
1964	16	1		11		

The above table is intended to give an indication of the evolution of services and omits trains run on less than five days a week. It includes through trains between the North of England and the South Coast, which were usually once a day, other than on summer Saturdays. Most other trains called at all stations, to meet local needs and to provide transport for the large number of ramblers from urban areas, seeking the joys of the Surrey countryside. From September 1957, a Reading train started from Gomshall at 7.44 am, and this service lasted until January 1965 by which time it originated at Dorking Town. From 4th January 1965, diesel-electric multiple units provided a regular interval hourly service (two-hourly on Sundays), calling at almost all stations between Reading and Tonbridge. Some additional trains were hauled by diesel locomotives until May 1977. On 12th May 1980, an hourly service was added between Reading and Gatwick Airport, mostly running non-stop between Guildford and Reigate, although Dorking (Deepdene) became a regular stop after 12th May 1986. The bad news that day was that the local service was reduced to one mid-day train between the peak hour journeys.

After threats of closure in the 1960s, the route has benefited from a revival of passenger figures in the 1980s but successive generations of railway managers have failed to promote the scenic delights of the journey.

By the mid-1930s, through working to London was undertaken by only one train per day, a situation which prevailed until cessation in January 1965.

Through services

In the period 1863 to 1866, a service was operated between Birkenhead, Reading and Redhill, where the train divided for Hastings and Dover. Through running was resumed in 1897, when coaches were worked between Liverpool Central and Folkestone Harbour. Stations in the Midlands and the North on the Great Western and Great Central routes were linked to South Coast resorts between Brighton and Margate via through coaches or entire trains running through Guildford and Redhill, the combinations of terminating towns varying over the years. In 1938, the train composed of coaches from Deal, Dover, Hastings, Eastbourne and Brighton was finally united at Redhill but on reaching Guildford it was split into portions for GWR destinations and for Bournemouth via Alton.

During much of WWII, a lengthy train operated between Ashford (Kent) and Newcastle, mainly for the benefit of service personnel. After the war, through holiday trains were resumed, with several passing in succession along the route on summer Saturdays. This useful facility was withdrawn in 1964, forcing non-car owners to travel via London. It remains to be seen if the route is to play any part in handling Channel Tunnel traffic. The need to reverse at Redhill is a serious problem in working through trains, this being well illustrated during the evacuation of troops from Dunkirk in 1940.

Reigate services

With the advent of electrification on 17th July 1932, the timetable improved enormously with the addition of a ½-hourly departure for London to the existing steam train service. At Redhill, these trains were attached to the Three Bridges portion, which was later extended to Brighton. Since 1966, through London trains have been restricted to the peak hours and only a few extra local journeys to Redhill have been made on weekdays, the Sunday ½-hourly service having been withdrawn in June 1963. In recent years, the local trips have been largely undertaken by DMUs for operational convenience, but the town still retains a good frequency as all Gatwick Airport trains call there.

GUILDFORD

1. The 1845 station was enlarged piecemeal and eventually rebuilt in the 1880s in the form seen here. Motor and horse drawn cabs are queuing to load under the ornate canopy or porte-cochère. After years of neglect, the buildings were demolished, early in 1988. (Lens of Sutton)

2. The brickwork to the right of the well-lagged water column had survived from the original station. The train is bound for Redhill on 21st April 1956, behind class D ex-SECR 4-4-0 no. 31549. (H.C. Casserley)

3. A class D1 stands at platform 5 on 14th September 1957, with a Reading to Redhill service. The platforms were re-numbered in 1938, thirteen years after a bay platform had been added for the new electric services on the Effingham Junction line. (D. Fereday Glenn)

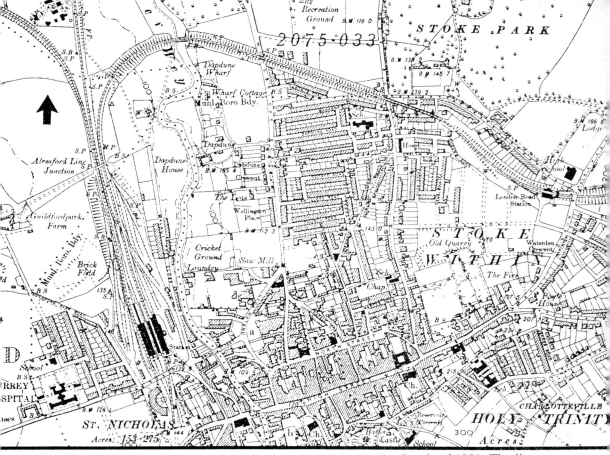

The 6″ to 1 mile map of 1897 includes both road bridges over the River Wey. The northern one was opened on 12th July 1882, to give a direct link between the station and North Street, where the cattle market was held. The county town was fortunate to have two bridges when the older one was damaged and closed during the floods of 1901. The line to Reading is on the left; to Woking at the top and to Effingham Junction on the right, while Portsmouth and Redhill trains enter the tunnel close to the final S of *ST. NICHOLAS*, near the bottom of the map.

4. Ex-GWR 2-6-0 no. 6302 waits at platforms 6 and 7 simultaneously on 15th February 1958 and attracts the attention of loco spotters, although Western Region engines regularly worked between Reading and Redhill. The proximity of the cylinders to the platform prevented the larger Western engines using most Southern routes.
(T. Wright)

5. The earlier length of platform 6 is shown by the change to brickwork, under the sign on the left. Class N 2-6-0 no. 31858 is in transit from Reading to Redhill on 3rd July 1963 and the gas holders in the background were soon to give way to commercial development. (T. Wright)

6. The close relationship of platform 8 to the coal stage is evident in this view from Farnham Road bridge on 18th June 1961. On the left, class 700 0-6-0 no. 30326 stands with the ash wagon and carries a motor registration plate (TPC707) together with an L plate!
(R.S. Greenwood)

7. No. 8 platform was not in use between 17th April 1966 and 26th April 1970. This is the scene on 18th March 1970, during the removal of the former middle siding. Subsequently, platform 8 has been used mainly for terminating trains from Waterloo via Aldershot. (R.E. Ruffell)

8. On 18th December 1973, the Bradford to Redhill parcels train was hauled by no. D7018 and is seen near the fence that was erected when platform 8 was shortened. (R.E. Ruffell)

9. In its final years, the main building had a redundant drinking fountain at its south end but a functional refreshment window at the other. This communicated with the buffet on platform 2. (C. Hall)

10. Platforms 4 to 8 are signalled for reversible running and all, except no. 8, can accommodate twelve coaches. This May 1987 view of a Reading bound train shows that platforms 7 and 8 had lost their canopy by then. (J.H. Bird)

Other views and maps of this station can be found in *Branch Lines to Horsham, Woking to Portsmouth* and *Reading to Guildford*.

11. Demolition was well advanced when this photograph was taken in July 1988. On the left is part of the 1938 footbridge and one of the arches over the subway. The barrows indicate that letter mail traffic was still an important part of the station's business – a nightly travelling post office service between Dover and Manchester was introduced in May 1988. (J.H. Bird)

12. Construction of the new £5.9m buildings and the raising of the platforms was progressing well, when recorded on 29th October 1988. Some considered progress to be slow but the cathedral, in the background, took proportionally longer – from 1936 to 1961. The train is standing in one of the two electrified berthing sidings. The footbridge is being renovated and new steps provided at platform 2. It will be for public use and not restricted to passengers. Plans are being made for buses to use the forecourt. (V. Mitchell)

13. The 18 roads of the engine shed radiated from the turntable, on which class Q1 no. 33019 is seen on 29th May 1961. Over the ash pit is the shed pilot, class B4 0–4–0T no. 30089. The roundhouse was opened in 1887, replacing a two-road building situated on the site of the north end of the present platforms 7 and 8. The straight part nearest the tunnel was added in 1896. (R.S. Greenwood)

14. After the extremely severe winter of 1962–63, BR was well prepared for trouble as class Q no. 30541 basks in the sun with its snowplough on 17th January 1964. The 50ft. turntable was operated by vacuum supplied from the locomotive's braking system. (R.E. Ruffell)

15. Class 4 no. 76032 accelerates towards South Box with the 12.05 pm Reading to Tonbridge service on 28th February 1964, as the Redhill to Woking freight emerges from the tunnel. It includes continental vans and Kent coal. The signal box was closed on 17th April 1966 when a new panel box superseded it. (R.E. Ruffell)

16. The N class was the typical motive power for the route for many years. Three examples take the morning sun on 24th August 1965 – nos. 31816, 31411 and 31866. The shed was closed with the end of steam on the Southern Region on 9th July 1967. (R.E. Ruffell)

17. The tunnel was shortened to 845 yds. during the construction of the locomotive shed but this portal was not built until over 50 years later. The 8.55 Tonbridge to Reading service emerges on 27th June 1969, formed of class 3D (now 207) unit no. 1303, one of 19 sets first introduced in 1962. (J. Scrace)

18. As at Reading, the station car parking crisis has been met with a multi-storey structure. The unusual method of construction, seen on 29th October 1988, included 15.6m long girders, bowed 250mm. The bowing was halved after the pouring of the concrete floor, the reinforcements of which were looped round the studs seen projecting from the steelwork. An exceptionally safe structure resulted – any spilt petrol would run off the floor and any impact to the frame would not result in floor slabs collapsing. (V. Mitchell)

19. The nearest train is the 12.40 Reading to Gatwick Airport seen on 23rd September 1986, having just emerged from the Chalk Tunnel. It is about to enter St. Catherine's Tunnel which passes through sand and which collapsed spectacularly in 1895 – see picture 31 in *Woking to Portsmouth*. (J. Scrace)

20. Viewed from the flood plain of the River Wey, class N no. 31870 is within sight of Shalford Junction, as it proceeds towards Redhill on 4th March 1961. The cutting leads to St. Catherine's Tunnel which was 132 yds. long luntil lengthened by about four yds. at its north end in 1984. The ruins of St. Catherine's are on the hilltop. (T. Wright)

21. Shalford Junction was of considerable strategic importance during World War II and the signal box was therefore protected from bomb blast by a casing of thick brickwork. The box was closed on 17th April 1966 after which the facing points were worked from Guildford Panel and the trailing points became self acting. Later they became power operated. (D. Cullum)

22. A lengthy freight train diverges from the Portsmouth line, destined for Redhill on 4th March 1961. Changing direction from south to east, the line descends slightly before crossing the River Wey, near the delightfully situated St. Catherine's Lock, so clearly seen from the train. (T. Wright)

A substantial bridge over the River Wey was constructed in timber and is viewed north from an embankment built to carry a connection between the SER and the LSWR, facing towards Portsmouth. The second bridge was built, again in timber, but it is doubtful whether track was ever laid across it.

23. The bridge was rebuilt in steel in 1912 and class no. 31620 is shown eastbound on it in May 1963. *Surrey Waterways* (Middleton Press) contains details of the Godalming Navigation and the Wey & Arun Navigation which diverged from the Wey Navigation ½ mile south of this bridge. (D. Vine)

SHALFORD

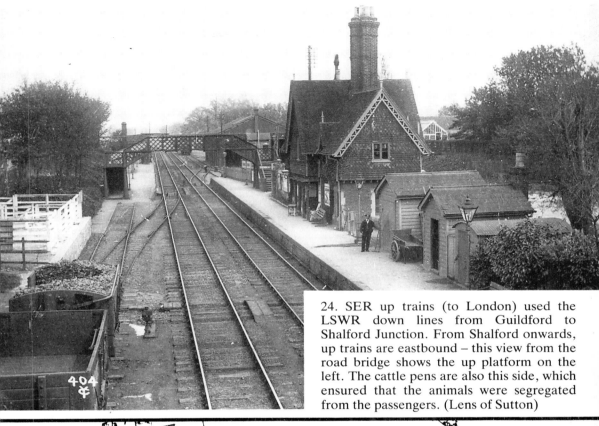

24. SER up trains (to London) used the LSWR down lines from Guildford to Shalford Junction. From Shalford onwards, up trains are eastbound – this view from the road bridge shows the up platform on the left. The cattle pens are also this side, which ensured that the animals were segregated from the passengers. (Lens of Sutton)

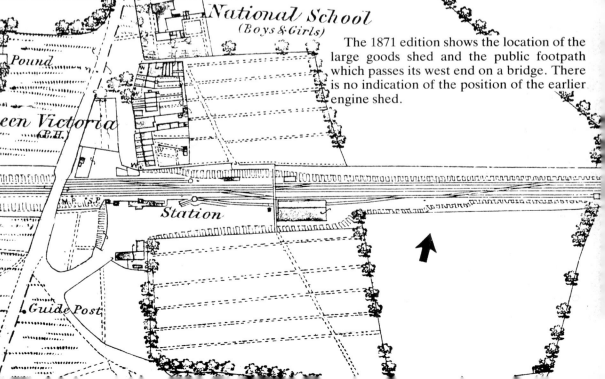

The 1871 edition shows the location of the large goods shed and the public footpath which passes its west end on a bridge. There is no indication of the position of the earlier engine shed.

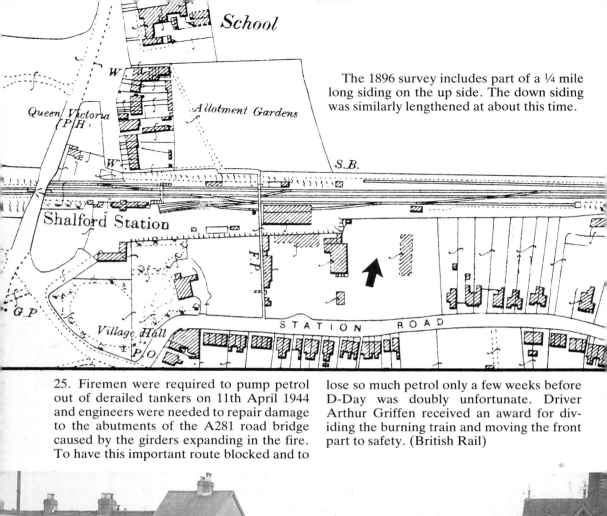

School

W

Queen Victoria P H

Allotment Gardens

W

S.B.

The 1896 survey includes part of a ¼ mile long siding on the up side. The down siding was similarly lengthened at about this time.

Shalford Station

F.P.

G.P.

P

Village Hall

P.O.

S T A T I O N   R O A D

25. Firemen were required to pump petrol out of derailed tankers on 11th April 1944 and engineers were needed to repair damage to the abutments of the A281 road bridge caused by the girders expanding in the fire. To have this important route blocked and to lose so much petrol only a few weeks before D-Day was doubly unfortunate. Driver Arthur Griffen received an award for dividing the burning train and moving the front part to safety. (British Rail)

ALFRED GITTINGS.
LICENSED POTATO VEGETABLE & FRUIT MERCHANT
WHOLESALE ONLY.   PHONE GUILDFORD 62222
Distributor of - KIRDFORD GROWERS LTD West Sussex Lights

NB
596

26. Refreshment was dispensed to men of the National Fire Service from a mobile canteen, a converted Rolls Royce which the photographer thought so unimportant that he omitted the radiator. Earlier in WWII, Shalford had been a sub-control for the railway part of the Dunkirk evacuation. (British Rail)

The WWII control diagram indicates the extent of the marshalling yard which was opened on 19th October 1941 to handle the increasing military traffic on the route. It was later used for mail vans and eventually became a permanent way depot, its final use being in connection with the Bournemouth electrification scheme in 1965–66. For a brief period, the yard was used as a locomotive depot when Guildford's turntable was out of action.

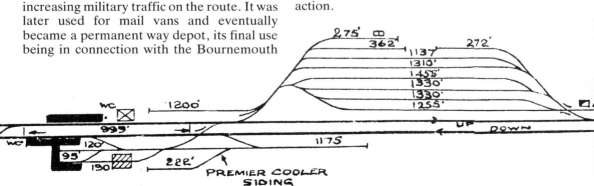

PREMIER COOLER SIDING

27. The tall chimneys and gables were typical of the other intermediate stations on the route, but unfortunately almost all has been lost in favour of a small glazed shelter. Staffing ceased on 5th November 1967, when conductor/guards were introduced. Just the toilets remain, for use by the road transport firm occupying the yard. (Lens of Sutton)

28. The unusual public footbridge spans the entire picture, as U class 2–6–0 no. 31616 arrives from Redhill on 11th June 1961. Part of the water column is visible at the end of the up platform, its tank still surviving in 1988 as the room under it was used by the trackmen. (R.S. Greenwood)

29. The passenger footbridge is viewed from the public footbridge on 7th March 1969, as a Tadpole unit arrives from Reading. These were so called as the driving trailer, nearest the camera, was wider than the two ex-Hastings line coaches. The site of the dock lines is being filled in, the goods yard having closed on 8th May 1967. (J. Scrace)

30. This signal box was opened on 28th February 1954 and was close to its predecessor. Eleven of its 28 levers remained in use in 1989, it then being the only intermediate box between Guildford and Reigate. The remaining siding was closed on 31st July 1987, its points being visible behind class 119 unit no. L580 on 13th October 1988. (C. Wilson)

31. East Shalford level crossing was provided with a gate box only. On the left of this 1951 picture is the east end of the marshalling yard, departure from which was controlled by a ground frame. The crossing is no longer in public use. (D. Cullum)

32. This gate box was situated on the down side, 1½ miles east of Shalford, until automatic half barriers were installed on 11th July 1974. In the background is the A248 from Shalford. (J. Scrace)

CHILWORTH

The 1897 survey is dominated by the large gunpowder works and its associated 2′7½″ (80cm.) gauge railway network, which linked it to the SER's single siding. Mill Race is clearly marked but the Tillingbourne is less obvious, being narrower and much bridged, in the northern part of the works. The East India Company established powder mills here in 1625 and Surrey soon became the main source of explosives in the country, the Chilworth Works expanding immensely. Until the advent of high explosives in the 1890s, the ingredients were 75% potassium nitrate (from India), 10% sulphur (from Italy) and 15% charcoal (produced locally). The works railway was extended to the SER goods yard in 1888, until which time all explosives were transported by punt and thence by barge from Shalford. After a number of changes of ownership, the Admiralty built a cordite works on the site in 1915, the works closing in 1920. The building near the world *Mill* contained a steam engine, as water power proved inadequate.

Gunpowder Mills

Weir

Chilworth

Guide Post

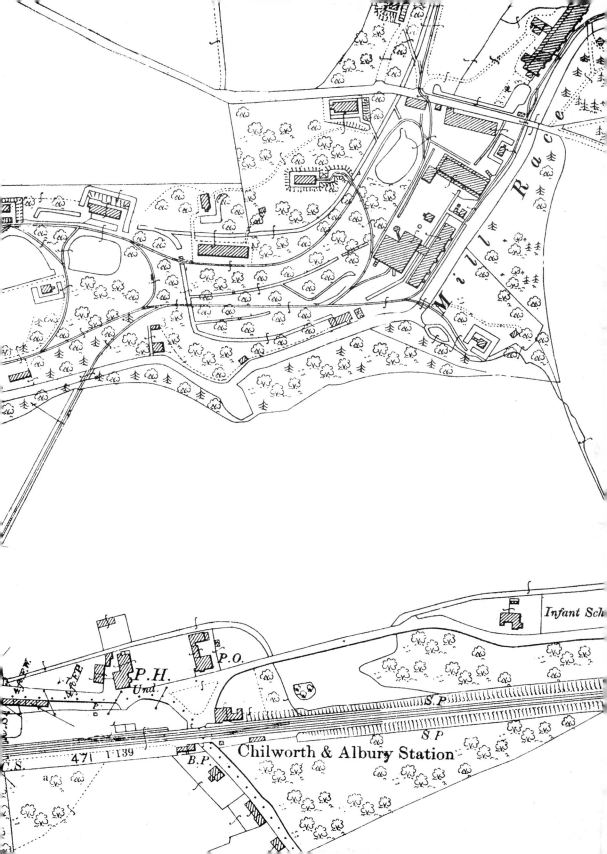

Mill Race

Infant Sch

P.O.

P.H.
Und.

S.P.

S.P.

471 1·139

Chilworth & Albury Station

C.S.

B.P.

33. Opened with the line as "Chilworth & Albury", the station has changed little over the years. The roadside canopy has been lost and the footbridge was moved to the East Somerset Railway, later being sent to Market Bosworth. The creeper-clad staff cottage on the right was painted white in its final years. (Lens of Sutton)

34. Looking west in 1935, we see the small level goods yard and the main line dropping at 1 in 100. The original length of the platforms is evident from the ramp to the extensions. Freight facilities were withdrawn on 7th May 1962. (Lens of Sutton)

35. Class F1 no. 1089 arrives from Guildford on 21st March 1936 with assorted vans preceding the coaches. The lines through the station were also on a gradient of 1 in 100, dangerously steep before the advent of continuous brakes. By the 1860s, 1 in 130 was the maximum permitted for new stations. (H.C. Casserley)

By the time of the 1934 edition, two more sidings had been laid and a 5-ton crane provided.

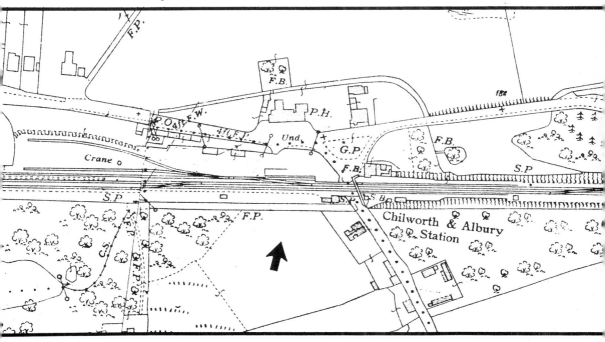

36. On the same day, a down train enters the station behind class U1 2-6-0 no. 1904. For some years, there was a short down siding between the lamp room at the end of the platform and the bridge in the distance. (H.C. Casserley)

37. The station ceased to be manned on 5th November 1967 and these shelters were erected for passengers. Type 3 no. 6551 roars up the bank with a stone train on 4th June 1970, having just crossed the A248, the gates being visible in the distance. (J. Scrace)

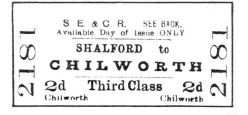

S E & C. R.   SEE BACK.
Available Day of Issue ONLY
SHALFORD to
CHILWORTH
2d   Third Class   2d
Chilworth   Chilworth
2181   2181

38. When photographed on 13th October 1988, class 117 DMU no. L420 was forming the 12.45 Redhill to Reading stopping service. At that time the station buildings were in use as offices and the signal box served as an office store, the box having lost its normal function when barriers (controlled from Shalford under CCTV) were brought into use on 9th June 1978. Chilworth gates were bought by the Dart Valley Railway. (C. Wilson)

39. Driver Heath and Fireman Earle climb to the summit on 4th September 1965, while working the Blisworth to Redhill parcels with U class 2–6–0 no. 31639. Above the right spectacle glass is a large pheasant standing on a chair. This topiary is a memorial to Guard Jesse, who died in an accident whilst on duty on a SER freight train. (R.E. Ruffell)

40. The last day of steam on the route was 2nd January 1965 and so the LCGB ran a special using U class 2–6–0 no. 31831. She is climbing hard past "Jesse's Seat", which is partly obscured by a telephone pole, In 1988, the topiary was sadly neglected. (S.C. Nash)

S. R.

CHILWORTH to
GOMSHALL & SHEIRE
4d   Third.   4d
Children over 3 and under 12 years
half fares, under 3 years free.
Gomshall   Gomshall

7056

41. Two miles east of Chilworth, on the long ascent of Albury Heath, the line passes Brook Crossing, seen here from the east. Note the vertical palings of the gates and the crossing keeper's small cottage.
(Lens of Sutton)

42. Brook Crossing Box ceased to be a block post in 1955 and closed totally on 19th July 1965, displaced by automatic half-barriers. Class N no. 31862 blows off as it drifts downhill on 5th November 1955, with the 10 am freight from Tonbridge to Scours Lane, Reading. (D. Cullum)

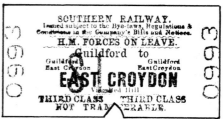

43. The 10.40 am Birmingham (Snow Hill) to Eastbourne curves vertically as it passes over the summit level, near milepost 36¼, on 22nd August 1953. In this case, the entire train is of Western Region origin. Shere Heath Bridge is in the background and is one mile from Gomshall. (S.C. Nash)

44. Class S15 no. 30837 is seen coasting over Gomshall Lane crossing on the same day, hauling the 3.35 pm Reading to Redhill service. The crossing was renamed Burrows Lane when automatic half barriers were commissioned on 14th April 1981. (S.C. Nash)

GOMSHALL

45. A westward view from about 1873 shows the main buildings on the up platform, round-ended wagons in the sidings, a wagon turntable and small signal box at the end of the down platform. (Lens of Sutton)

The 1934 map shows that no sidings existed on the down side at that time. The sand pit served for Home Guard rifle practice during WWII. 2½ miles to the east, a wooden halt for Westcott Rifle Range was in use between 1916 and 1928. A signal box was nearby, on the down side, until 13th March 1935. A mile to the west of it, Evelyn's siding was on the up side, serving a limeworks between October 1926 and July 1940.

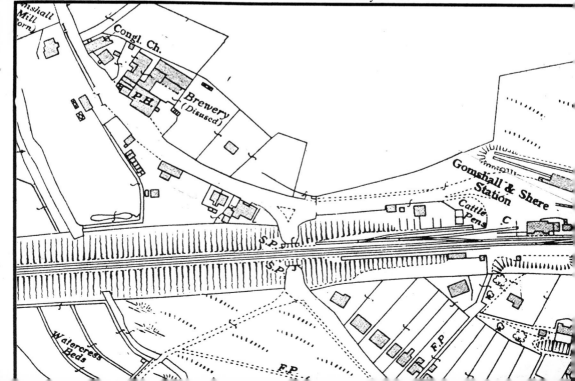

46. A spectacular derailment took place on 11th February 1903, involving O class 0–6–0 no. 284 which was hauling a troop train of LSWR coaches, from Woolwich Arsenal to Portsmouth. Amazingly, there were no fatalities. (Lens of Sutton)

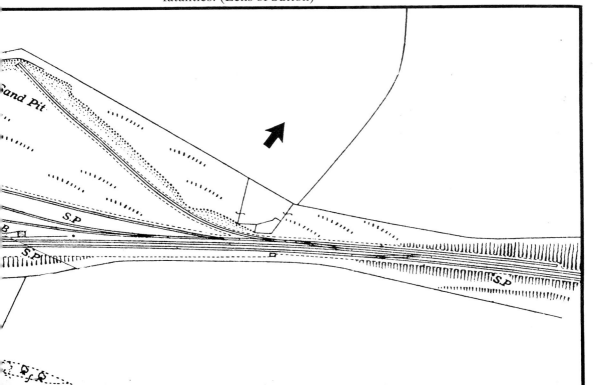

47. The motor vehicles would date this view as after about 1920, when the signal box was still beyond the crossover. The semaphore ground signals seldom appear clearly in photographs. Churns of milk and baskets of watercress were notable goods despatched, one or two of the latter sometimes being seen on the tender. (Lens of Sutton)

49. Ex-LSWR class T9 no. 30120 is seen working the 4.20pm Reading to Redhill train on 22nd August 1953. The ex-SECR Bird-cage sets were commonly used on local trains on this route for several decades. An example can be seen on the Bluebell Railway, while the locomotive can now be found on the Mid-Hants Railway. (S.C. Nash)

48. A plethora of luggage barrows have gathered round the station master's tiny office, which was created in the original signal box. This 1953 westward view includes the SR style of ground signal for comparison with the earlier type. (D. Cullum)

S. E. & C. R,
Available Day of Issue ONLY.
GOMSHALL & Shere to
REIGATE
1/10   First Class   1/10
Reigate   Reigate
See back

086   086

50. Down graded main line coaches of Maunsell's design for the London – Hastings line were often used in the final years of steam. A Morris Minor GPO van waits by the crossing as N class no. 31405 comes to a halt with the 12.35 from Redhill on 31st July 1964. (J. Scrace)

52. The signal box was closed on 6th December 1980 but was still in use by the Permanent Way Dept. when photographed on 19th May 1988, as DMU no. L588 was departing for Redhill at 16.29. The goods shed was also extant, the yard being used as a caravan sales ground. As at Ham Street, passengers still crossed the line on the level. (V. Mitchell)

British Railways Board (S)

GOMSHALL & SHERE

PLATFORM TICKET 3d.

Available one hour on day of issue only.
Not valid in trains. Not transferable.
To be given up when leaving platform.
For conditions see over

0003   0003

51. The 4-ton crane was functionless when photographed in 1964, as goods facilities had ceased on 10th September 1962. A new signal box was opened on 26th October 1941, as the previous one had been damaged by enemy action, and a down loop was added at the same time. (J. Scrace)

"Welcome Bridge" is at the summit of the line and was so called by footplate crews for obvious reasons. It carried the lane from the A25 to Effingham and was of unusual iron construction with wooden decking and palings but it has since been rebuilt in brick and concrete. (R.E. Ruffell)

Top right –
53. The route has carried many unusual trains in both war and peace. No. 33059 hauls the coaches of the Venice Simplon Orient Express, on a special from Victoria to Ascot on 27th July 1985. Some of the first concrete sleepers on the SR were laid on the up line in this area near Ranmore Common, but they were not a success. (J. Scrace)

54. On the outskirts of Dorking on 15th May 1979, Tadpole unit no. 1204 failed while working the 17.04 from Redhill. The following DEMU is seen coupled to it, prior to pushing it to Guildford. In the background is St. Martin's Church, unusual in that the churchyard has no street frontage.
(W. Walker)

DORKING WEST

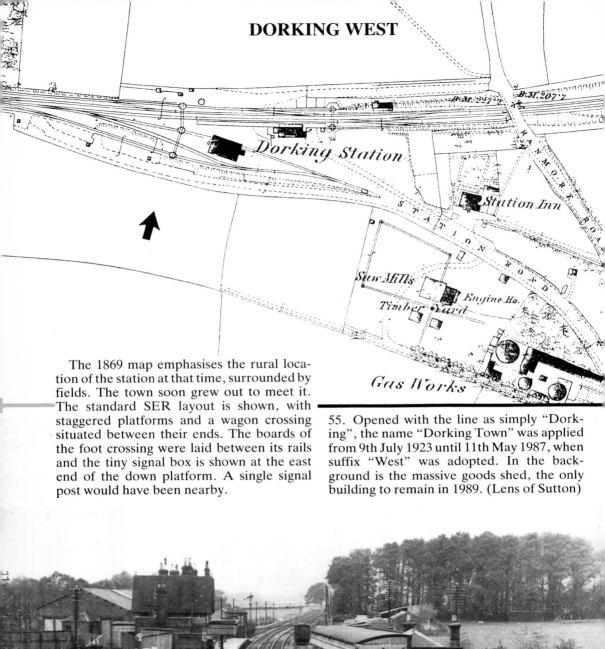

The 1869 map emphasises the rural location of the station at that time, surrounded by fields. The town soon grew out to meet it. The standard SER layout is shown, with staggered platforms and a wagon crossing situated between their ends. The boards of the foot crossing were laid between its rails and the tiny signal box is shown at the east end of the down platform. A single signal post would have been nearby.

55. Opened with the line as simply "Dorking", the name "Dorking Town" was applied from 9th July 1923 until 11th May 1987, when suffix "West" was adopted. In the background is the massive goods shed, the only building to remain in 1989. (Lens of Sutton)

56. A WWI news photograph includes MR and LNWR freight vehicles in the goods yard, and also shows the end-loading dock, used for loading or unloading agricultural equipment and horse-drawn vehicles. Note the unconventional hanging of the doors on the right pillar. (Lens of Sutton)

57. Dorking has lost most of its historic buildings, along with its mediaeval poultry market which was noted for its five-toed chickens. This historic building, photographed in April 1950, was swept away in December 1969, having been unstaffed for two years. (D. Cullum Collection)

58. With the North Downs in the background, class E 4–4–0 no. 31315 passes the 8-ton crane in May 1952, as it approaches the up platform. The view is now marred by a car breaker's yard. Goods facilities were withdrawn on 6th May 1963. (D. Clayton)

59. A Birdcage set passes under Ranmore Road bridge a few minutes later, hauled by ex-LSWR class T9 no. 30307. The first-class saloon in the coach on the left had the luxury of individual armchairs. The siding was the headshunt for the dock road. (D. Clayton)

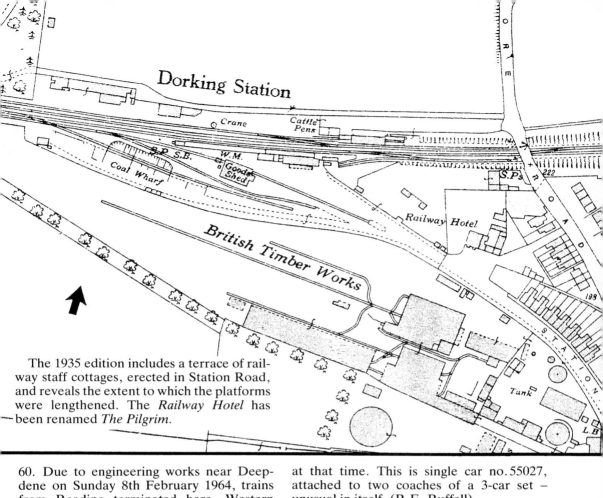

Dorking Station

Crane

Cattle Pens

S.P. S.B.

W.M.

Coal Wharf

Goods Shed

British Timber Works

Railway Hotel

S.Ps

222

198

STATION ROAD

Tank

L.B

The 1935 edition includes a terrace of railway staff cottages, erected in Station Road, and reveals the extent to which the platforms were lengthened. The *Railway Hotel* has been renamed *The Pilgrim*.

60. Due to engineering works near Deepdene on Sunday 8th February 1964, trains from Reading terminated here. Western Region DMUs were uncommon on the route at that time. This is single car no. 55027, attached to two coaches of a 3-car set – unusual in itself. (R.E. Ruffell)

61. The up platform shows evidence of extension and also carries a banner repeater signal, as the canopy obscured the view of the starting signal. The up siding was added in about 1850, in connection with the building of Denbies, a large country mansion on Ranmore Common. (Lens of Sutton)

Further information can be found in Alan A. Jackson's *Dorking's Railways* (ISBN 1 870912 01 2 Dorking Museum)

62. A photograph from 30th June 1969 shows that the signals had gone and that the platform lighting was in transition. The subway was added in 1885 and the curved roofs over the steps were still in place in 1989. (J. Scrace)

63. Part of the goods shed and the subway entrances can be seen in this view from Ranmore Road of no. 33012 heading the 11.38 Woking to Tonbridge ballast train, on 13th October 1988. (C. Wilson)

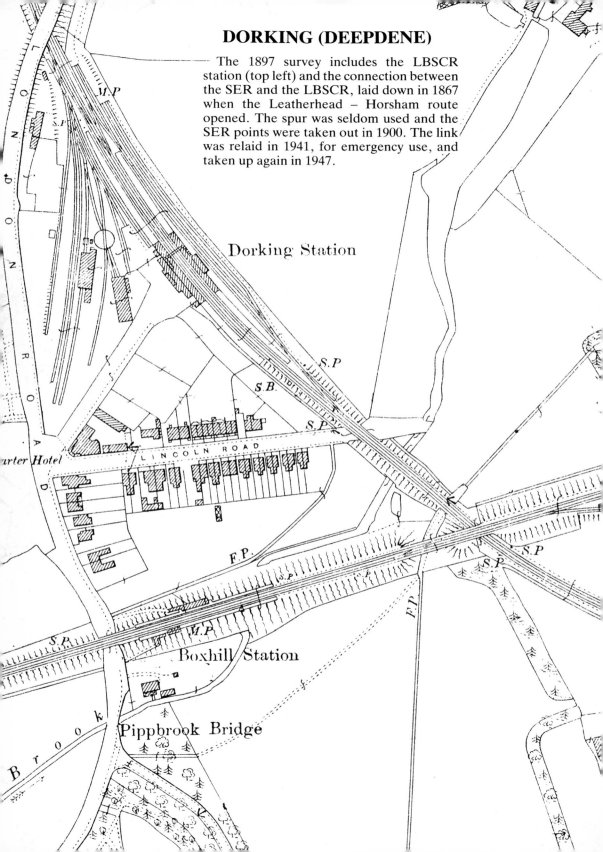

DORKING (DEEPDENE)

The 1897 survey includes the LBSCR station (top left) and the connection between the SER and the LBSCR, laid down in 1867 when the Leatherhead – Horsham route opened. The spur was seldom used and the SER points were taken out in 1900. The link was relaid in 1941, for emergency use, and taken up again in 1947.

Dorking Station

Lincoln Road

arter Hotel

Boxhill Station

Pippbrook Bridge

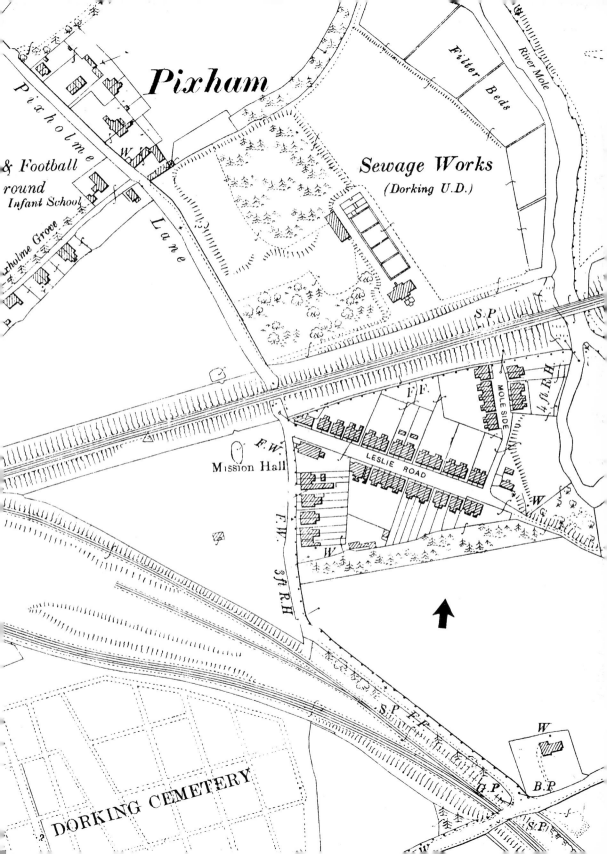

64. Brought into use early in 1851 as "Box Hill & Leatherhead Road", the suffix was soon dropped as the bus service failed to materialise. The name was changed to "Deepdene" on 9th July 1923 and to "Dorking (Deepdene)" on 11th May 1987. From May 1986 Gatwick Airport trains called regularly. This Edwardian postcard gives a rare view of the signal box, which was demolished in the early 1920's. (Lens of Sutton)

65. Being built on an embankment, construction was of timber to reduce weight. Steps gave access to the main buildings on the up side, passengers for down trains using a foot crossing at the west end of the platforms or steps up from the road. (Lens of Sutton)

66. The staff adopt the customary pose as class F no. 60 arrives from Redhill, amid a prolific display of enamelled advertisement signs. Construction problems were compounded by the presence of Pipp Brook passing under the far end of the platforms. (Lens of Sutton)

67. Westbound class F1, numbered A79 by the SR, is about to pass across the brick arch over the A24 on 18th March 1928. The line climbs at 1 in 100 for ¾ mile to Dorking Town station. (H.C. Casserley)

69. The 07.24 Reading to Tonbridge service approaches on 24th September 1968, composed of Tadpole unit no. 1203. The station is boarded up, prior to its demolition at the end of 1969. (J. Scrace)

68. The ever popular recreational area of Box Hill appears in this 1963 eastward view. In steam days, it was an ideal location for a binoculared railway observer, as exhaust steam could be traced through woodland for miles, on two routes. The parapets of the bridge over a footpath and the Horsham line are visible beyond the platforms, but those of the five-arched viaduct over the River Mole are not. (E. Wilmshurst)

70. A photograph from 21st March 1987 indicates the present width of the A24, following the removal of the narrow brick arch that carried the railway until 1964. Steel steps, regrettably devoid of roofs, are now provided from road level to each platform. Unit no. L581 displays the extensive area provided for luggage when in use on Gatwick Airport services. (A. Dasi-Sutton)

71. Class N 2–6–0 no. 31400 passes over the Horsham line with the 12.35 Redhill to Reading train on 30th April 1964, as it approaches Deepdene. The running main lines are on the right, the next is the down loop, the one on the left being a carriage siding. (J. Scrace)

Details of Dorking North station can be found in our *Epsom to Horsham* album.

72. Built as a country mansion, "The Deepdene" became a hotel in the 1920s and was purchased in 1938 by the SR, to serve as their wartime headquarters. Communication with divisional offices was by despatch riders, who used Austin 10s, 12s and motorcycles, and by wireless, the equipment often being fitted into road parcel vans. Further details can be found in *War on the Line*, reprinted by Middleton Press. The building ceased to be used as railway offices in 1966 and was demolished in 1968. (R. Randell Collection)

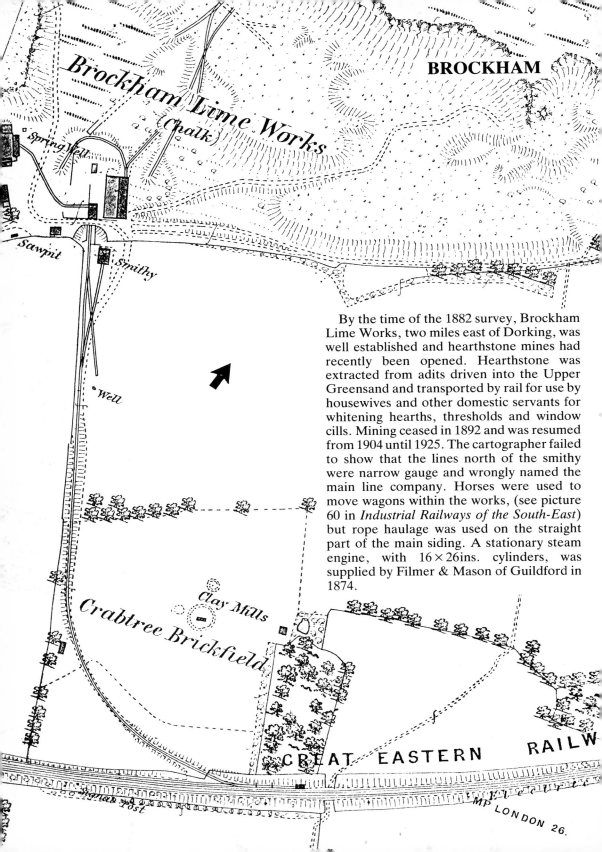

BROCKHAM

By the time of the 1882 survey, Brockham Lime Works, two miles east of Dorking, was well established and hearthstone mines had recently been opened. Hearthstone was extracted from adits driven into the Upper Greensand and transported by rail for use by housewives and other domestic servants for whitening hearths, thresholds and window cills. Mining ceased in 1892 and was resumed from 1904 until 1925. The cartographer failed to show that the lines north of the smithy were narrow gauge and wrongly named the main line company. Horses were used to move wagons within the works, (see picture 60 in *Industrial Railways of the South-East*) but rope haulage was used on the straight part of the main siding. A stationary steam engine, with 16×26 ins. cylinders, was supplied by Filmer & Mason of Guildford in 1874.

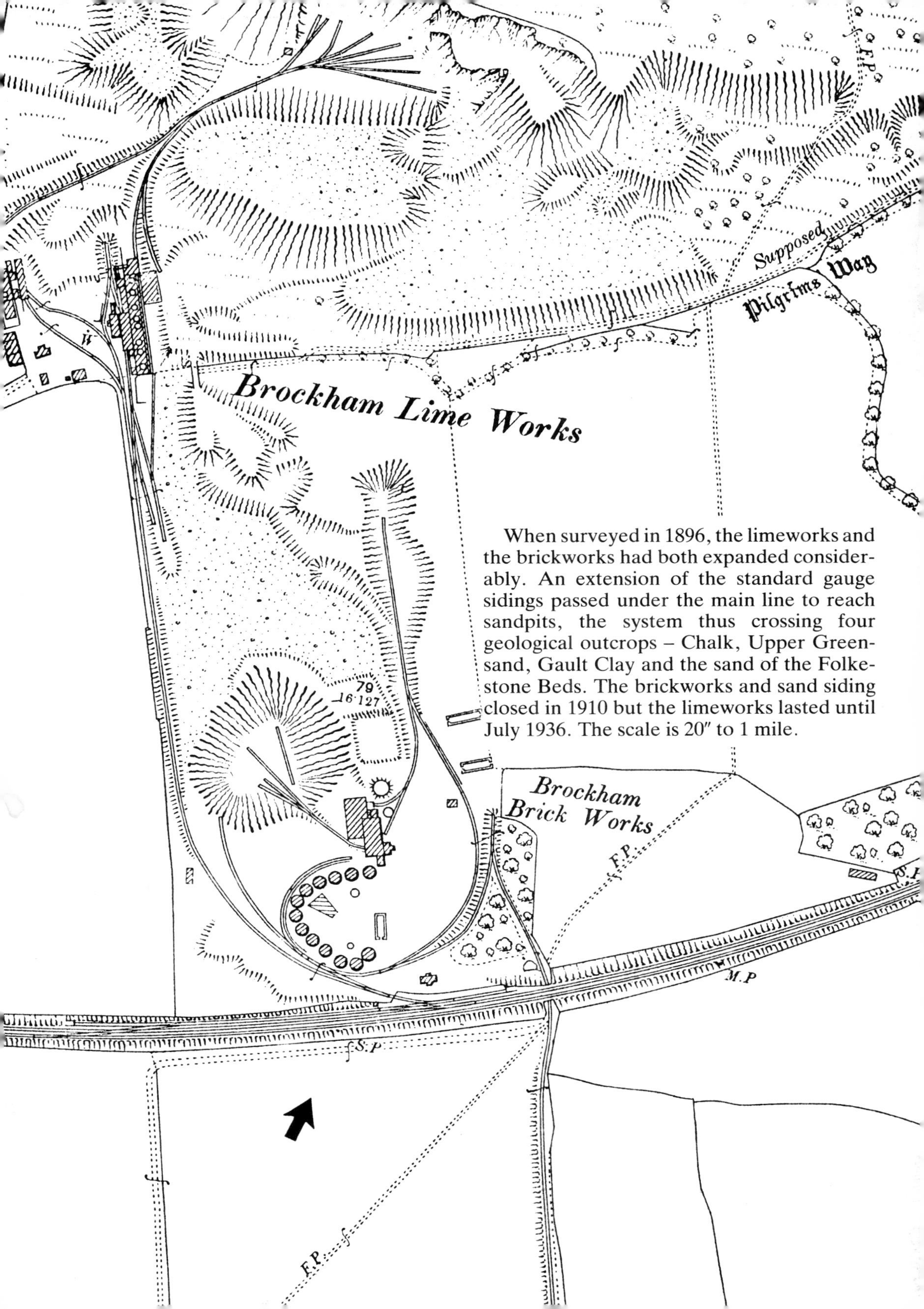

Brockham Lime Works

Supposed Pilgrims Way

When surveyed in 1896, the limeworks and the brickworks had both expanded considerably. An extension of the standard gauge sidings passed under the main line to reach sandpits, the system thus crossing four geological outcrops – Chalk, Upper Greensand, Gault Clay and the sand of the Folkestone Beds. The brickworks and sand siding closed in 1910 but the limeworks lasted until July 1936. The scale is 20″ to 1 mile.

Brockham Brick Works

79
16·127

F.P.

M.P.

S.P.

F.P.

73. In 1962, a museum of narrow gauge industrial railways was established and by 1979 it had six steam and eleven i.c. locomotives, together with a wide range of other stock. Ex-Betchworth Quarry Orenstein & Koppel *The Major* is seen in use on the 2ft gauge demonstration track in 1975. Owing to planning and access problems, the entire collection was moved in 1984 to the Chalk Pits Museum at Amberley in West Sussex, where it is available to a wider public. (A.C. Mott)

74. Brockham Crossing gave access to the quarry and was manually operated until automatic half barriers were fitted on 5th June 1983. Schools class no. 30907 *Dulwich* speeds west on 5th January 1960, destination Reading. (D. Knapman)

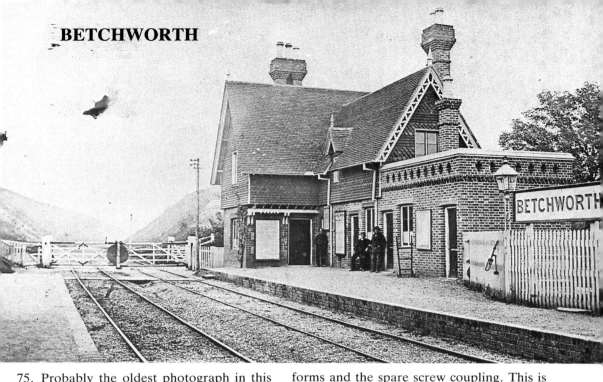

BETCHWORTH

75. Probably the oldest photograph in this album, it does not show the signal post marked on the 1871 map. Note the low platforms and the spare screw coupling. This is one of the six intermediate stations opened with the line. (Betchworth collection)

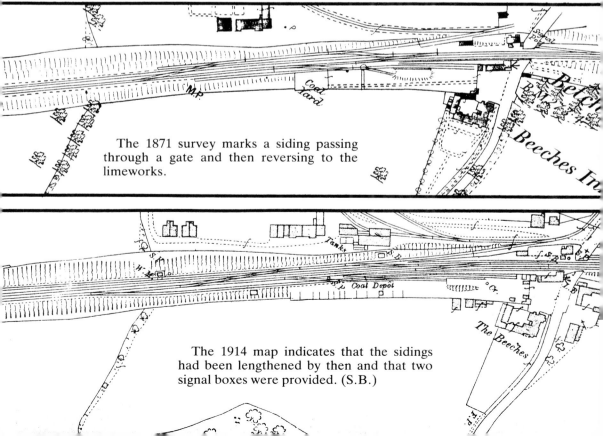

The 1871 survey marks a siding passing through a gate and then reversing to the limeworks.

The 1914 map indicates that the sidings had been lengthened by then and that two signal boxes were provided. (S.B.)

76. This view includes a signal box close to the level crossing and wagons in the short up siding beyond it. Ballasting over the sleepers could hide rotten ones and was eventually forbidden. (Betchworth collection)

77. The crossover was mainly used during freight movements and so could occupy an unusual position, between platforms. C class no. A225 arrives from Guildford on 20th August 1932, showing the headcode for London. (H.C. Casserley)

78. LMS and GW wagons stand on the limeworks line as U class no. 1798 departs east on 9th November 1935. Beyond the level crossing is the short goods dock with its single cattle pen. (H.C. Casserley)

79. Class D no. 31496 passes the wagon weighbridge with the 1.31pm from Redhill on 23rd April 1955. In addition to discs, it is showing a tail lamp, a common practice among Redhill crews. (J.J. Smith)

80. Green painted Western Region 2–6–0 no. 5341 gleamed in the evening sun as she departed with the 4.04pm Redhill to Reading train on 8th June 1957. The grass-covered headshunt in the foreground was still in place over 30 years later. (J.J. Smith)

81. Freight traffic was in decline as class C2X 0-6-0 no. 32450 departed for Redhill with a solitary wagon from the nearby limeworks, on 4th July 1959. No exit sign was provided, only a message to gentlemen. (D. Knapman)

82. On 12th April 1934, both signal boxes were closed and operations transferred to the booking office, seen on the right. The rodding tunnel is visible by the leading wheels of class N no. 31863 which is arriving with the 5.34pm from Redhill on 11th May 1963. (E. Wilmshurst)

83. This ground frame was provided at the end of the down platform to control access to the sidings, authorisation for movements being made by the signalman in the booking office. The main line drops at 1 in 116, the headshunt on the right being level.
(D. Knapman)

84. This fine view of the North Downs and the 6½-ton crane was taken shortly after freight facilities were withdrawn on 28th September 1964. It seems that the coal merchant had stocked up well before being forced to obtain supplies by road. (J. Scrace)

85. The architectural style of the former inn was almost as flamboyant as the station itself, a number of details being found in SER stations elsewhere. This 1988 picture includes the barriers, controlled under CCTV from Reigate. They were installed on 20th November 1977 and were operated from the adjacent box until its closure on 5th June 1983. (V. Mitchell)

BETCHWORTH QUARRY

The extent of the Dorking Greystone Lime Company's various lines in about 1955 is shown in relation to the three pits and the one mine worked at that time. The firm operated four different gauges, the 1'7" being hand worked into the hearthstone mine. Bridges are shown for carrying the Pilgrims Way and the lines used for charging the kiln batteries. (Brockham Museum Association)

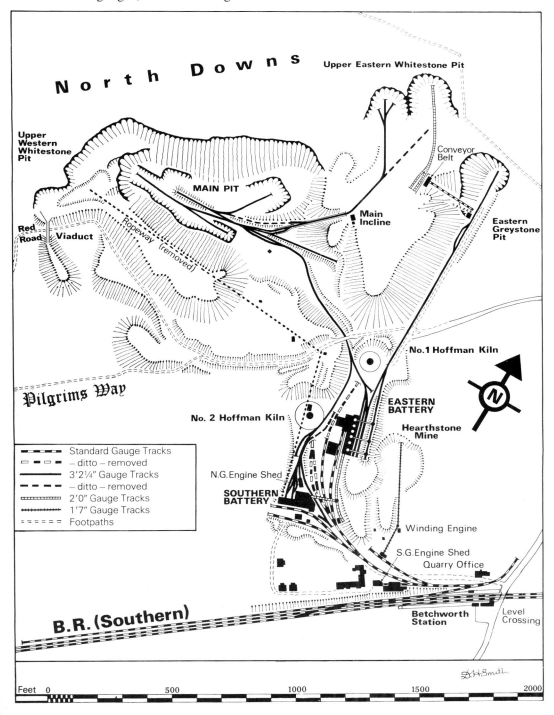

Legend:

- Standard Gauge Tracks
- – ditto – removed
- 3'2¼" Gauge Tracks
- – ditto – removed
- 2'0" Gauge Tracks
- 1'7" Gauge Tracks
- Footpaths

86. The quarry was started in 1865 when a connection was made to a siding on the SER. This is seen in the foreground, with the main line to Reigate in the background. (D. Cullum collection)

87. This is a 1959 view in the opposite direction and includes the BR down platform and boundary gate on the left, the line to the quarry centre and the quarry access road on the right. This road was completely obstructed during shunting operations.
(D. Knapman)

88. Standard gauge shunting was mainly carried out by two locomotives during the life of the works, two others being only transitory. This is no. 1, unofficially named *The Coffeepot* and built by T.H. Head in 1871 and now at Beamish, County Durham. Until that time, wagons were moved individually by a team of eight horses. (P. Hay)

| 0182 | SOUTHERN RAILWAY.
ONE DOG AT OWNER'S RISK (accompanied by Passenger)
Deepdene to
3ᴰ any Station on the SOUTHERN RAILWAY
not exceeding 10 miles
This ticket is available for one journey only and must be given up at destination Station.
FOR CONDIT⋯IS SEE BACK | 0182 |

| 055 | S. E. & C. R. (SEE BACK)
Available Day of Issue ONLY.
Betchworth to
COULSDON & CANE HILL
1/3 Third Class 1/3
Coulsdon Coulsdon | 055 |

89. Another 1953 photograph features no. 3 *Baxter*, the other standard gauge shunter. Constructed by Fletcher, Jennings & Co. in Whitehaven in 1877, it was the last engine to steam on the line when it closed in 1960. It is seen running down towards the station and is now preserved on the Bluebell Railway. (P. Hay)

90. There were two steam locomotives for the 3′2¼″ gauge system, both manufactured by Fletcher Jennings in 1880. No. 4 *Townsend Hook* is seen on 2nd April 1952. In the background is the no. 3 Dietzch kiln and the chimney of the no. 2 Hoffman kiln, by then both long disused. The management was noted for its innovation. (D. Clayton)

91. *Townsend Hook* was named after a former chairman of the Dorking Greystone Lime Co. Ltd., owners of the quarry. This engine, along with no. 5 and both diesel engines, can be seen at the Chalk Pits Museum at Amberley. The eastern battery is in the background. (D. Clayton)

92. No. 5 *William Finlay* was named after the founder of the firm, who had previously been a resident engineer during the construction of the Nord Railway and the Manchester, Sheffield and Lincolnshire Railway. It is returning to the quarry face in July 1953. (P. Hay)

93. The main incline was worked in a novel manner. The locomotive at the bottom was attached to the wagon by a lengthy steel rope which passed round two pulleys. As the engine reversed, two tons of chalk was gently lowered to its level. (P. Hay)

For further photographs and maps of Brockham and Betchworth Quarries, see *Industrial Railways of the South East,* **(Middleton Press, reprinted 1989) and** *Townsend Hook and the Railways of the Dorking Greystone Lime Co.* (0 950472 04 2 Chalk Pits Museum)

94. ½ mile east of Betchworth, Buckland Crossing is provided to serve Kemp's Farm and adjacent dwellings. It is seen from the south in 1975, when the sign on the gate read *RING FOR GATEKEEPER*. Automatic half barriers were brought into use on 27th February 1980 and nine years later the cottage was still the home of a railwayman, the sole remaining such dwelling on the route. (D. Cullum)

95. Buckland siding was one mile east of the crossing, on the up side, and prior to WWII connected with a 2ft gauge line which passed under the main line to run for ½ mile south to the pits of the Buckland Sand & Silica Co. Their locomotive is shown in picture 119 of *Industrial Railways of the South East*. During the war, additional sidings were laid north of the main line to serve a large store for ammunition and canned petrol. Their final use was by the coal merchants, Charringtons. (J. Powell)

96. A signal box and up loop were provided during WWII. The railings are on the bridge over Clifton Lane. Both pictures were taken in the late 1960s, the previous one from the steps of this box. The former Government buildings were later used for the storage of theatrical scenery. (J. Powell)

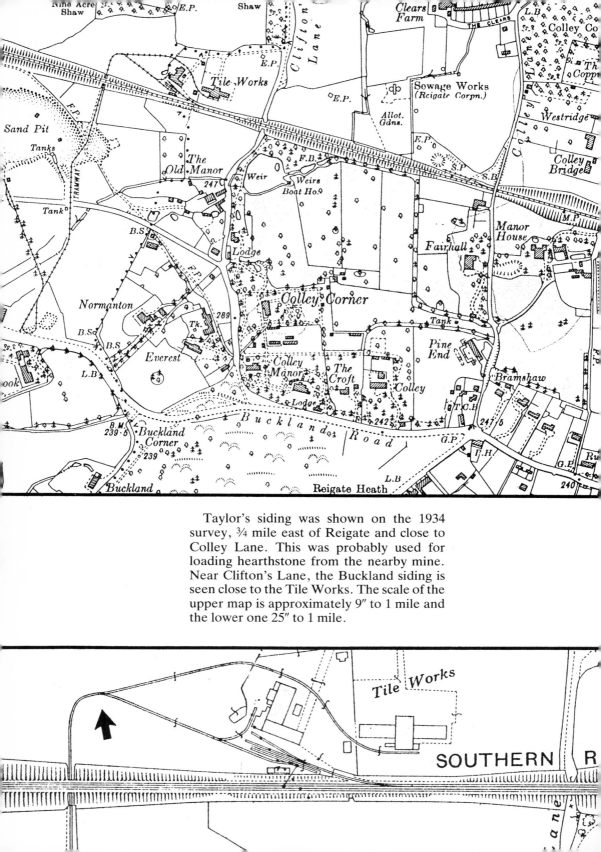

Taylor's siding was shown on the 1934 survey, ¾ mile east of Reigate and close to Colley Lane. This was probably used for loading hearthstone from the nearby mine. Near Clifton's Lane, the Buckland siding is seen close to the Tile Works. The scale of the upper map is approximately 9″ to 1 mile and the lower one 25″ to 1 mile.

REIGATE

97. Known as "Reigate Town" until 1898, this sadly damaged print shows the station before extension of the up platform eliminated the sidings on the left. In the background we see *The Prince of Wales* (left), the signal box (centre) and the goods shed on the right. The picture was probably taken from a signal post as the footbridge is not in view. (H.J. Snook/J. Powell collection)

98. The platforms and canopies were extended in about 1907. A timber-clad signal box, with sash windows and a gate wheel, was erected but the crossing cottage remained, eventually to be replaced by a row of small shops. (Lens of Sutton)

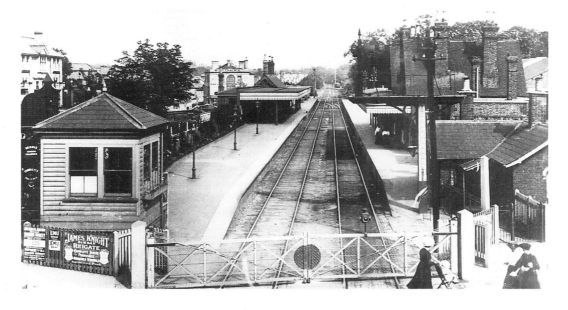

99. The curved roof behind the lamp post on the left covers the subway steps. The 1895 footbridge in the background is for public use. As a wartime economy measure, the station was closed from 1st January 1917 until 1st February 1919. (Lens of Sutton)

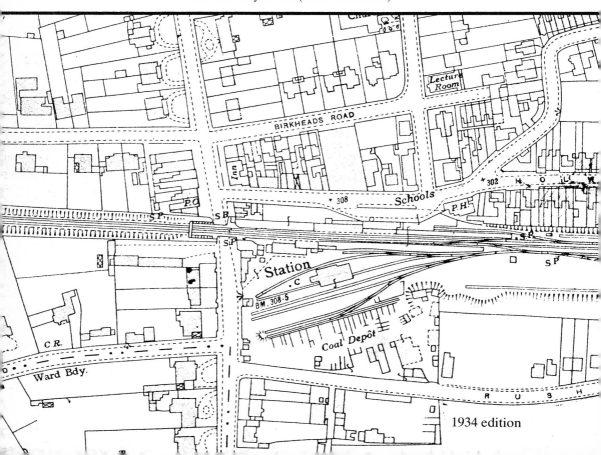

1934 edition

100. The motor car age had arrived, although it is not immediately obvious. Signs proclaim GARAGE at the tip of the left whip and above the recipient's head. Brighton-bound trippers in their horseless carriages were soon to cause such difficulty for the signalman trying to close the gates, that the constabulary had to attend the proceedings regularly at summer weekends. (H.J. Snook/ J. Powell collection)

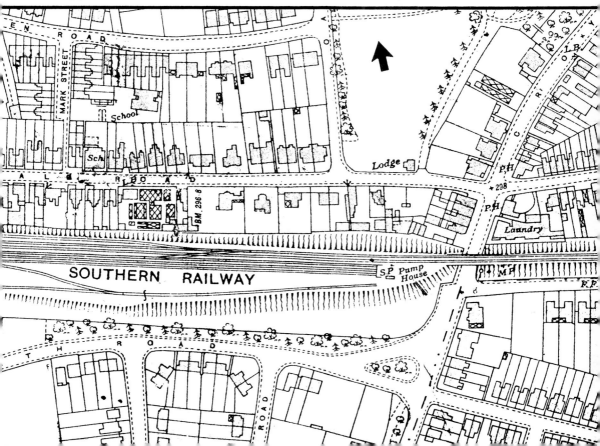

101. The conductor rail reached the level crossing in 1932, regular services commencing on 17th July as part of the Brighton electrification scheme. The complete sign on the left read *NO EXIT THIS WAY*. The signal box was provided by the SR in 1930, replacing those seen in pictures nos. 97 and 98. (Lens of Sutton)

102. Due to engineering works on 22nd March 1959, the electric service was replaced by a push-pull unit, seen arriving from Redhill via the up line. One of the sidings was electrified – later there were three. The goods yard was located behind the camera and was closed on 28th September 1964, the shed remaining until 1984. (S.C. Nash)

103. D7088 heads the 11.35 am Redhill to Reading on 14th December 1963, during the transition period from steam haulage. During this time, it was necessary for diesel locomotives to provide steam heating for the coaches, but not necessarily for the track. (E. Wilmshurst)

104. A 1969 photograph of the south facade shows that it was residential, a booking office being retained on the up side. In 1988, this was only staffed in the mornings. (J. Scrace)

105. The local service between Redhill and Reigate has been predominantly electrically operated in some years and diesel operated in others. The ground signal is off, ready for L574 to return to Redhill at 19.42 on 7th July 1981. Note that at that time there was one electrified siding and that the canopies had been reduced in length. (A. Dasi - Sutton)

106. In 1983, there was an hourly electric service – hence the shining conductor rail. This is the 10.20 departure for Charing Cross on 23rd January. For many years, 2 BILs had been the usual stock for this branch service. (A. Dasi - Sutton)

107. 33026 heads west with an engineer's train on 4th March 1988 and gives us the opportunity to see the re-arrangement of the berthing sidings. Since May 1988, stock could no longer be left overnight, owing to the high incidence of vandalism. (J. Petley)

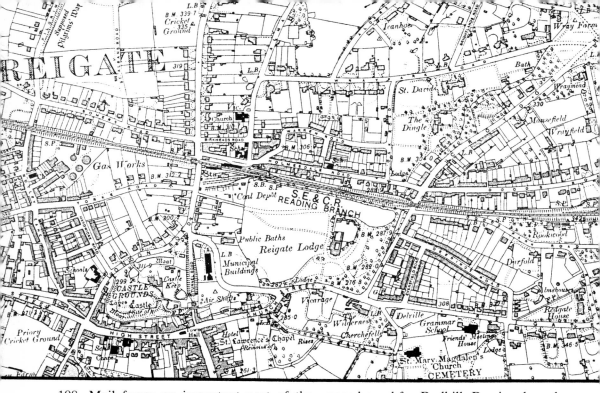

108. Mail forms an important part of the traffic on the route, as illustrated on 23rd August 1988 when no. 31415 passed by with vans bound for Redhill. Barriers have been in action here since 8th June 1969. (A. Dasi - Sutton)

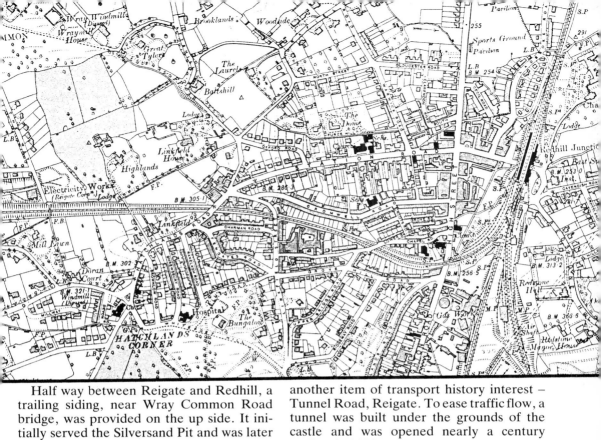

Half way between Reigate and Redhill, a trailing siding, near Wray Common Road bridge, was provided on the up side. It initially served the Silversand Pit and was later extended to Reigate Electricity Works. It is shown on this 1920 map at 6″ to 1 mile, as is

½ mile from Redhill, Bacon's siding was situated between Linkfield Street and Lower Bridge Road. It carried bones and hides for

another item of transport history interest – Tunnel Road, Reigate. To ease traffic flow, a tunnel was built under the grounds of the castle and was opened nearly a century earlier, in 1824.

the tannery, which is shown on this 1913 map.

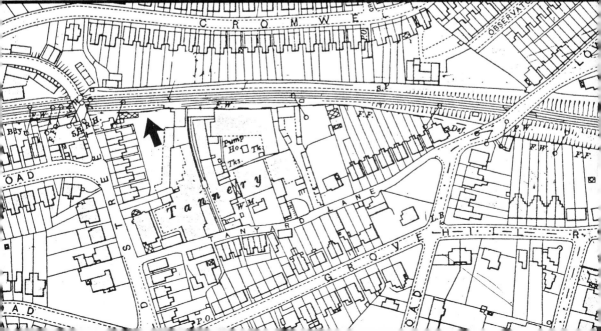

109. The former SER goods shed comes into view as class U no. 31639 rounds the 11 chain curve on the bridge over the High Street, which becomes Brighton Road at this point. The Blisworth parcels is signalled into platform 2 on 4th September 1965. (R.E. Ruffell)

2nd- DAY RETURN

8398

Cannon Street
London Bridge
or Victoria
TO
GOMSHALL
and SHEER
Via Redhill
(S) Fare 9/6
For conditions see over

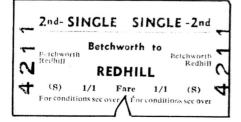

2nd- SINGLE   SINGLE -2nd

Betchworth to

4211   Betchworth
Redhill   Betchworth
Redhill
REDHILL
(S)   1/1   Fare   1/1   (S)
For conditions see over   for conditions see over
4211

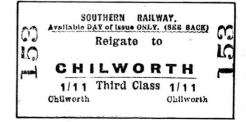

SOUTHERN RAILWAY.
Available DAY of issue ONLY. (SEE BACK)

03
153
Reigate   to

CHILWORTH
1/11 Third Class 1/11
Chilworth   Chilworth

REDHILL

110. Looking north from the southern signal box (no.2, later 'B'), we see the Reigate lines on the left and, in the centre, a train entering platform 2 from the Brighton direction. The flat wagon at the rear could be used for conveyance of a passenger's horse-drawn carriage. (E. Jackson collection)

111. A view south in the summer of 1913, shows the Reigate lines curving to the right of the signal box. East-west services have to reverse in the station, a feature which caused considerable congestion during the two World Wars, notably during the evacuation of Dunkirk (D. Cullum collection)

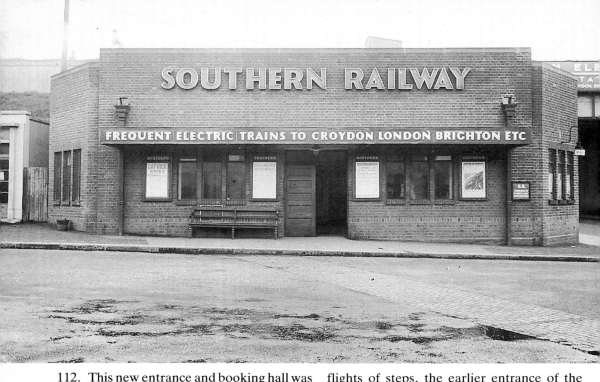

112. This new entrance and booking hall was built in 1930 in readiness for the increased traffic which would follow electrification. Access to the platforms is by way of two steep flights of steps, the earlier entrance of the down side being limited to staff use. (British Rail)

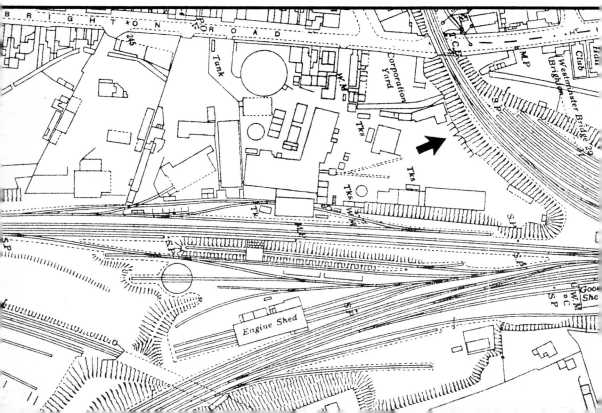

113. Holiday trains in the summers following WWII brought additional work at this awkward junction. Swindon built no. 5364 arrives with the 10.30 am from Birmingham (Snow Hill) on 11th June 1949, the coaches being taken forward to Eastbourne. It was followed 15 minutes later by the Birkenhead -Hastings service. (S.C. Nash)

The lines from Reigate are at the top of this 1933 map, the Brighton ones are on the left and those from Tonbridge are at the bottom. The first SER station was near the lower border of the map and the initial Brighton one was off the left page. These were closed in 1844 and a combined station was opened by the SER on the site of the present station, shown on the right page. It was known as "Reigate" until becoming "Reigate Junction" in 1858, when it was largely rebuilt. Thereafter it became "Redhill Junction", the suffix officially being dropped in 1929.

114. Activity at the north end of the station was recorded in May 1951. On the left, vans are shunted in or out of the Post Office bay, which was added in about 1930. In the foreground, a Birdcage set is being drawn towards platform 1, to work a service to Tonbridge or Reading. During WWII, 'A' Box, on the left, had an anti-aircraft gun installed on its roof. (D. Clayton)

S. E. & C. R. (SEE BACK)
Available Day of issue ONLY.

Reigate to

RED HILL

3d   Second Class   3d
Red Hill   Red Hill

7783   7783

116. One of the ubiquitous N class has just arrived at platform 1 from Reading, on 10th June 1961. At that time the narrow platform became seriously congested with the conflicting movements of passengers and barrows of mailbags. (R.S. Greenwood)

115. Viewed from behind 'B' Box in September 1957, class T9 leaves with the 1.31 pm to Reading, where it was due at 3.18 pm. Note the vast tonnage of point rodding that was required in the days of mechanical operation. (P. Hay)

117. The structure on the skyline reduced the barrow traffic on the platform – it contains an endless conveyor for mailbags, which passes above the main lines, direct into the sorting office. On 25th April 1973, the 16.40 departure for Reading was hauled by no. 6571. The sidings contain much sand, discharged by defective wagons from the nearby sandpits. (J. Scrace)

118. The 4VEP is bound for Reigate from platform 3 on 7th January 1984. As there was not room for two starting signals, a semicircular route indicator was provided. Since 12th May 1985, full colour light signalling has been operative, controlled from Three Bridges. (P.G. Barnes)

119. The skyline of Redhill changes yet again as the F&W Railtour's "Darkle Dungeneer" rounds the curve from Reigate on 28th July 1985, behind nos. 56047 and 56049. The train originated at Plymouth and was bound for Dungeness. (A. Dasi - Sutton)

Other views of stations on the route are included in Peter Hay's *Steaming through Surrey* and further pictures and maps of Redhill, including its locomotive shed, are shown in our *East Croydon to Three Bridges* album.

120. Seldom seen so far south, three class 20s (no. 20064, 20030 and 20118) return to Sheffield from Brighton on 2nd May 1987. Twelve months later Redhill was to have a permanent connection with the Midland line when the hourly Bedford - Brighton service commenced, using pantograph-fitted class 319 units. (C. Wilson)

MP Middleton Press

Easebourne Lane, Midhurst, West Sussex, GU29 9AZ
☎ Midhurst (073 081) 3169

BRANCH LINES
BRANCH LINES TO MIDHURST
BRANCH LINES TO HORSHAM
BRANCH LINES TO ALTON
BRANCH LINE TO HAYLING
BRANCH LINE TO SOUTHWOLD
BRANCH LINE TO TENTERDEN
BRANCH LINES TO NEWPORT
BRANCH LINES TO TUNBRIDGE WELLS
BRANCH LINE TO SWANAGE
BRANCH LINES TO LONGMOOR
BRANCH LINES TO LYME REGIS
BRANCH LINES **AROUND** MIDHURST
BRANCH LINE TO FAIRFORD
BRANCH LINE TO ALLHALLOWS

SOUTH COAST RAILWAYS
CHICHESTER TO PORTSMOUTH
BRIGHTON TO EASTBOURNE
RYDE TO VENTNOR
EASTBOURNE TO HASTINGS
PORTSMOUTH TO SOUTHAMPTON
HASTINGS TO ASHFORD*
SOUTHAMPTON TO BOURNEMOUTH
ASHFORD TO DOVER
BOURNEMOUTH TO WEYMOUTH

STEAMING THROUGH
STEAMING THROUGH KENT
STEAMING THROUGH EAST HANTS
STEAMING THROUGH SURREY
STEAMING THROUGH WEST SUSSEX
STEAMING THROUGH THE
   ISLE OF WIGHT

SOUTHERN MAIN LINES
WOKING TO PORTSMOUTH
HAYWARDS HEATH TO SEAFORD
EPSOM TO HORSHAM
CRAWLEY TO LITTLEHAMPTON
THREE BRIDGES TO BRIGHTON
WATERLOO TO WOKING
VICTORIA TO EAST CROYDON
TONBRIDGE TO HASTINGS
EAST CROYDON TO THREE BRIDGES
WOKING TO SOUTHAMPTON
WATERLOO TO WINDSOR
LONDON BRIDGE TO EAST CROYDON

COUNTRY RAILWAY ROUTES
BATH TO EVERCREECH JUNCTION
BOURNEMOUTH TO EVERCREECH JUNCTION
READING TO GUILDFORD
WOKING TO ALTON
GUILDFORD TO REDHILL

OTHER RAILWAY BOOKS
WAR ON THE LINE
(Reprint of the SR history in World War II)
GARRAWAY FATHER AND SON
(Biography - includes LNER, Talyllyn and Festiniog Railways)
INDUSTRIAL RAILWAYS OF THE SOUTH-EAST

OTHER BOOKS
MIDHURST TOWN – THEN & NOW
EAST GRINSTEAD – THEN & NOW
THE MILITARY DEFENCE OF WEST SUSSEX
WEST SUSSEX WATERWAYS
SURREY WATERWAYS
BATTLE OVER PORTSMOUTH
A City at war in 1940
SUSSEX POLICE FORCES

*Video also available. Details from
M.P. Videos, 11 Park Crescent, Midhurst,
West Sussex GU29 9ED.*